CW01661758

TAKE THE PLUNGE

HOW TO DIVE INTO VENDOR MANAGEMENT AND ENJOY IT

By Carmen Cisneros

Editing by Turquoise Tiger Press

Graphic design by Mhd Mohsin - Behance @Colour Nation

Illustrations by Jen Du - Instagram @jendu

TURQUOISE TIGER PRESS

Edited by Turquoise Tiger Press, Lincolnshire, UK

Copyright © 2022 by Carmen Cisneros

All Rights Reserved

No part of this book may be reproduced or transmitted in any form by any means: graphic, electronic, or mechanical, including photocopying, recording, taping or by any information storage or retrieval system without permission, in writing, from the author, except for the inclusion of brief quotations in a review, article, book or academic paper. The author, editor and publisher of this book and the associated materials have used their best efforts in preparing this material. The author, editor and publisher make no representations or warranties with respect to accuracy, applicability, fitness or completeness of the contents of this material. They disclaim any warranties, expressed or implied, merchantability, or fitness for any particular purpose. The author, editor and publisher shall in no event be held liable for any loss or other damages, including, but not limited to special, incidental, consequential or other damages.

Manufactured in the United Kingdom.

ISBN: 978-1-7398221-1-8

To everyone who helped me be
the person that I am today.

"Therefore, vendor recruitment must be counted among the most critical of processes for translation firms. After all, organisations can work with the most up-to-date technology and design the most intricate of production processes, yet even with the best supporting components in place, the translation product will only be as good as the translator who provides the target content."

—Alaina Brantner, The ATA Chronicle (2017)

Table of Contents

Before Diving in

We could say that vendor management has been seen as the dark horse of the language services industry, probably in a similar way to how purchasing and procurement are perceived in other industries.

Until very recently, company owners knew that a vendor management team was something many companies had, but they weren't fully aware of the real value that the team could add to the success of their business. Why's that? Because it doesn't bring in clients, and therefore, money, in the same way other departments do, such as sales or project management. This means they would only use the help of a vendor manager when other roles within the company could not absorb the responsibilities often associated with the vendor management team.

In fact, most of my professional career has been introducing or updating processes related to vendor management and tidying up vendor databases after months of neglect in different companies. Implementing new procedures and cleaning up the database are not easy tasks that take months when working alone.

I think this was one of the main reasons why I wanted to write this book. I see vendor management as a core asset to a successful language services company, a team that can help build a business from the ground up and not a function that comes in once the company is up and running.

Luckily, this unenlightened view of the vendor management function has changed in the last couple of years, and nowadays, most companies realise that having a good vendor management team can boost their company's performance and add a lot of value to its services.

As the industry matures and grows, so do the number of organisations offering vendor management training worldwide, the amount of literature available and the number of events mentioning or dedicated to vendor management, answering the need to document best practice and guide newcomers into the industry.

Since the start of my professional career, I have always wanted to be involved in vendor management and the language services industry. I remember seeing my senior colleagues at Xerox's offices in England and Budapest back in 2014 and thinking "I want to do what they do". Vendor management wasn't taught as part of a translation course, at least not the one I attended back in 2008, and there wasn't much literature about the role widely available. I was resourceful enough to find a few useful presentations and articles by Cecilia Iros and Alaina Brantner, which helped immensely at the time.

Therefore, when I started my first role in vendor management in 2016, my boss's knowledge and my daily work were my only guide. In my free time, I tried to find webinars, articles and books that could help me understand the industry and the role better, but I couldn't find much specifically designed for the language services industry. I researched the web and read anything and everything about supply chain management, negotiation, procurement, and purchasing. I took what I could from other industries and applied it to the way we do vendor management in our world. If this book was available back then, my learning would have been much more straightforward.

It was then when I learned about the huge gap between language service providers (LSPs) and freelance vendors and the bias that existed between the two sectors. From companies paying their vendors last, and often late, without any concern for the safety of their business, to vendors sending abusive emails to company employees guarded behind their screen, I knew there had to be another way. Since then, it is my personal mission to bridge this gap and help both sides understand each other a bit better.

I always say that those two years I spent at Webcertain (a Transperfect company) helped me learn all the basics of the way I do vendor management now. I have kept growing and learning since then, working for different companies in different countries and this book is the result of my experience and career so far.

By the time this book is published, I will have been a vendor manager for six years, working in small, medium and large language service providers (LSPs) based in the United Kingdom, Hungary, Poland and America. Although I was worried about how this erratic career path would look on my CV, I knew I had to acquire a wider picture of the industry and how different companies operate so I could be a good vendor manager before starting to write this book.

A few years ago, I felt the need to fill the gap in training for vendor managers and I started a LinkedIn group that is now flourishing called Translation Vendor Management. This is a group for anyone and everyone interested in Vendor Management in the language services industry. A safe space where we share ideas, ask questions and learn from one another. Thanks to all the connections I have made through this group and my industry colleagues, I have learned about vendor management from the point of view of the end client, recruitment for multimedia services and even how interpreting departments work.

I believe this book is one of a kind and very much needed for any vendor management team and LSP worldwide, especially now that the industry is going through major changes such as the wide adaptation of technology by most companies and freelancers, an open discussion about the gap between companies and vendors, and the surge of investment from private capital in the industry.

If you are new to the vendor management world, this book is for you. If your company needs a brand-new vendor management team, this book is for you. If you want to learn more about vendor management, this book is for you.

Maybe you want to train your team of new vendor managers, but you are short on time. Give them this book! They will be able to understand the principles of the work of vendor management, and familiarise themselves with best practices used in the industry. It will save you time and make sure your team is respecting and valuing your vendors, while keeping in mind the company's policies and objectives.

According to the Merriam-Webster dictionary, *taking the plunge* means to do or undertake something, especially after a period of hesitation or uncertainty. This book will help you stop hesitating and safely dive into vendor management in the language services industry, while enjoying it! The book and I will give you a 360-view of the vendor management function - from the big picture to the smallest details.

Starting with an introduction to the language services industry and the vendor management function, we will move to the different responsibilities of the vendor management team: from recruitment, and management of vendors to tasks related to any vendor database. You will read about communication with vendors, business relationships, conflict resolution and negotiation. We will guide you through widely accepted best practices in the industry and encourage you to add your own touch to standard, bullet-proof vendor management processes used all over the world. All this illustrated with examples taken from my experience and the experience of colleagues which will help you navigate situations you may encounter.

I wanted to make this book enjoyable and informative, so my advice is to read it in short intervals. Give yourself time to integrate the knowledge and get the most out of it. Keep it nearby on your desk or read it on your way to the office, but most of all refer to it multiple times, take notes, underline and highlight as much as you need to so you can apply all these principles while going through your everyday tasks. Check out the blank pages for notes at the end of the book!

I promise you, no page has been wasted.

Chapter 1

Checking the Depth: Introducing Our Industry

1.1. Introduction to the Language Services Industry

To define the language services industry, I would like to take a quote from Renato Beninatto and Tucker Johnson's book The General Theory of the Translation Company. Their book is also one of a kind and I am sure it will keep helping newcomers to the industry years after it has been published.

"The language services industry includes any and all business related to helping language services buyers to adapt or create content, products or services in order to better compete in the global marketplace". So, any company providing translation, machine translation post-editing, multilingual voiceover, multilingual desktop publishing, transcreation, interpreting, among other services, would be part of the language services industry.

Although the act of translating from one language to another has been happening for a very long time, this industry is relatively young, and studies show that it continues to grow and change every year. During the last decade, the industry has seen a sustained growth: from 28 million US dollars in 2011, reaching over USD 51 billion in 2021, and it is expected to grow at a compound annual growth rate of six per cent from 2020 to 2028.

I use LinkedIn daily, and it is my preferred professional networking site right now. I did some research on this platform and found some interesting data. Before looking at the figures, I wanted to mention that I am aware these numbers are not fully accurate as there are countries where LinkedIn is not universally available. However, they are reliable enough to give you an idea of the spread of the members of the language services industry.

According to LinkedIn (Autumn 2021), there are 31,000 companies in the industry worldwide, of which 45% are in Europe and the Middle East, 37.5% in America, 17.5% in the Asia-Pacific region. Although it looks like most companies are based in Europe and USA, many medium-size and large companies have several offices located across time zones in different regions to offer a continuous service to their clients. When I worked at Akorbi in 2021, the vendor management team consisted of people working from South America, India and Europe, and the company had offices located in the USA, South America, India and Africa.

During my research on LinkedIn, I also found there are around 600,000 profiles under the Translation and Localization category and more than 160 job adverts across different platforms at the moment. These are often entry-level jobs in LSPs as well as adverts to recruit freelance vendors – as the industry keeps expanding, it needs a high number of new people coming into the industry.

I found it interesting that, according to a study done in 2018, there are around 1,800 LSPs in the UK and about 100 new translation and localisation companies are created each year. These figures are quite mind-blowing and, believe it or not, the industry is not highly concentrated. You might already be aware of the biggest companies out there such as Transperfect, Lionbridge, and RWS. According to a 2020 study, these companies make up only 7.6% of the entire revenue of the industry, 4.3 billion US dollars. This is because even though there are many LSPs out there, not all of them have the same aim in the market: whilst some focus on a small group of language combinations, maybe from a specific region or specialise in one subject matter, e.g. medical or patents, others tend to take on as many different jobs as they are offered. This way a client could work with one vendor, usually a LSP, that can provide all the services they need, or choose to collaborate with several vendors that could be LSPs or freelancers, each specialising in a different service. There isn't a rule about which approach is best, but in my experience, most large companies requiring language services prefer to work with different vendors and give each of them a part of the work they have got available.

The language services industry works as a supply chain, which means different roles come together to add value to meet a client's requests. The client might contact one LSP, that might outsource the job to another LSP, that can outsource the job to a freelancer. Obviously, this is an example of a simple cycle and there could be several variations, depending on the project.

Let's see an example of how the project cycle usually works for a translation request: the client will send a request for a task to be carried out, the LSP will assess the files and advise the client what needs to be done, depending on factors such as the format of the file, the purpose of the content and the languages involved. Once this is agreed, the text will go to a freelancer for translation, most probably with the help of a CAT (Computer Assisted Translation) tool, then to the reviser for the quality assessment stage, which looks at the macro and microstructures of the text.

There might be other services involved in the cycle such as desktop publishing, monolingual proofreading, or keyword insertion, depending on the final purpose of the text. Once these stages are completed, the LSP will send the translated text back to the client.

Many companies work in a Business Management System (BMS) which they use as a platform to save all their client information, vendor information and for tracking projects and payments. This way of working is becoming increasingly popular nowadays as companies move onto more automatic processes to make their workflow more efficient. Therefore, they can cope with the maximum amount of work in the shortest possible time, which in the industry is usually called being agile. This has led the industry towards machine translation, and automation of processes. However, overall, the language services industry is still very much dependent on human relationships, internally with company employees as well as when outsourcing tasks, especially for the vendor management team.

An example of automation gone wrong is mass emailing which is very much frowned upon nowadays, but that used to be the norm when I started my career. Sending the same email to more than ten vendors can be very time-consuming, and to be able to cope with the fast-paced environment, project managers and vendor managers are used to sending mass emails to dozens of email addresses in blind copy (BCC). After a few years, vendors started ignoring such emails and would openly discuss their annoyance at companies that used this practice to recruit or allocate projects, so much so that many colleagues have stopped using it and I always warn anyone from trying it out. I suggest using mail merge instead which allows you to add vendor names to each email.

As you can imagine, our industry is very much deadline-driven, and it can be very fast-paced at times. This is because of the chain workflow we follow - the fact that if one of the stages gets delayed, it affects the entire project as well as the final deadline.

Another consequence of the growth of our industry is that more and more businesses and governmental bodies are employing freelancers and LSPs on a regular basis, boosted by globalisation and the Great Resignation phenomenon. At the same time, universities that before only taught linguistics or cultural studies, now offer translation and interpreting courses to students all over the world. Employees are allowed to work from almost anywhere and strive to find a job and follow a career that suits them the best. Many choose to become freelance vendors because of the flexibility and lucrative potential.

The industry has also been investing in the development of language technology to automate and optimise company processes and drive the growth and continuous success of its industry members, like you and me. At the time of writing this book, main industry developments include multimillion dollar mergers and acquisitions, the booming of virtual interpreting, and the automatization of services such as subtitling, transcription and voiceover.

This is another reason why this was the best time to write the book you hold in your hands. I wanted to plant a seed with my unique take on our industry and vendor management, and see it bloom, together with the many advances happening in the language services industry now and in the future.

1.2. Introduction to the Structure of Language Service Providers (LSPs)

Let's have a look at the different roles in the language services industry. The roles and responsibilities shown here are quite generalised and simplified to give an overall idea of the inner workings of an LSP. However, according to the company's structure and objective, these job responsibilities and interactions among teams might change. For example, in smaller companies and start-ups, different roles might share some responsibilities to be cost-effective as some teams might not yet exist.

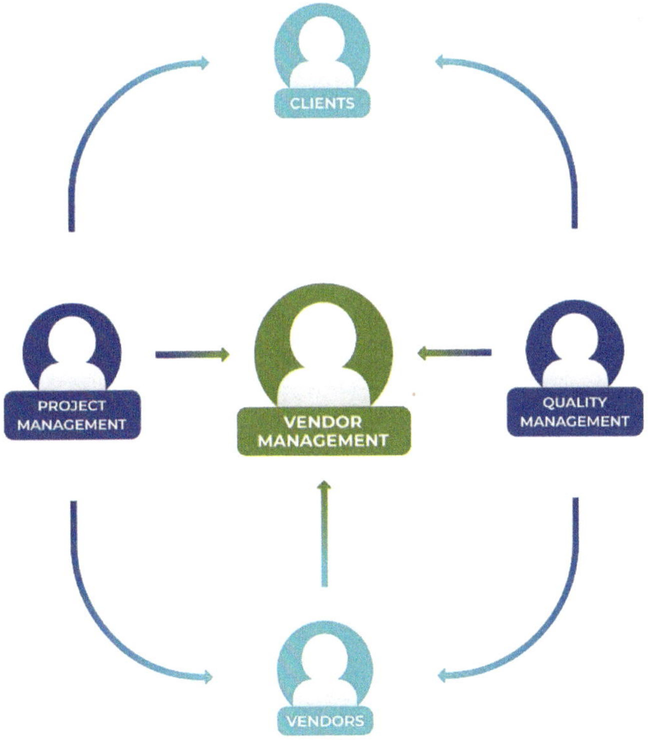

Vendors refers to all the vendors in a company's database. That could be freelance vendors, but also other LSPs able to provide useful services for the company.

Then, we have the vendor management team - the main point of contact for vendors, that also supports the project management team and the quality management team when necessary.

The project management team is the main point of contact for clients and focuses on getting the job done and achieving client satisfaction.

The quality management team monitors the vendors' performance and ensures the reference material and the quality of the content delivered to the client is up to the company's quality standards.

A very important team, in my opinion, is the localisation engineers that take care of all the technical aspects of the process such as data management, file conversion, and software troubleshooting.

Last, but not least, we have back-office roles that include sales, human resources, finances, and IT support teams, among others. These are teams that every company needs at some point of their development to be able to function effectively.

If you want to learn more about the localisation industry and how language service providers (LSPs) work, I recommend The General Theory of the Translation Company book mentioned earlier. It's full of detailed industry information, including how LSPs operate. I like it because it highlights project management, vendor management and sales as the core functions of any company in the language services industry. I strongly agree with this categorisation, as I have seen many companies not being able to develop their full potential after having neglected their vendor management function (their vendors), focusing only on sales and project management (their clients). When I started my career, more experienced colleagues told wild tales of rumours of vendor managers who had taken confidential data on their last day of work and founded whole new successful companies using it. I haven't seen this happening in a real scenario, but it highlights the fact that a company's database and its vendor management team are the foundation of a company.

Considering a practical approach, not investing in a good vendor management team from the beginning can translate into a company recruiting vendors reactively in a rush according to the requests they might receive, instead of ensuring a steady flow of services from their vendors by being proactive. This mistake can risk quality, service standards and their reputation.

It is important to note that project management, vendor management and quality management teams are interconnected and should always work together to ensure the project meets a client's expectations. This is a key component for any successful company, however, it doesn't always come naturally or easily for their team members. In my opinion, pro-activeness and clear communication are vital for a successful internal collaboration.

While Project Management takes charge of communication with the client and the smooth running of a project's life cycle, vendor management is responsible for ensuring the best vendor is ready to be used for different tasks and quality management ensures reference material is relevant and content quality is up to a client's standards.

Quality management and vendor management work together to ensure the vendors' performance complies with the company's standards. The quality management team performs checks on the vendors' output and sends them any feedback available, while the vendor management team makes sure the database is updated and reflects the vendors' strengths and opportunities for improvement.

Project management and vendor management collaborate to ensure vendors are being offered projects that align with their skills and that they are available for new projects whenever needed. The vendor management team can also help project managers plan future projects in advance and project managers can support the vendor management team by giving them feedback on the vendors' overall performance on a regular basis.

The structure of the LSPs' internal teams can vary, but it usually follows one of the following models: division by location, process or service. This means the company might want to create several groups across teams to take care of the clients/vendors located in different regions around the world: Europe, America, Middle East, Africa. In this model, the LSP might employ project managers, vendor managers and quality managers in different locations and time zones and assign a group of clients and vendors to work with regularly. On the other hand, it might make more sense for the company to split them by industry such as life sciences, manufacturing, multimedia, etc. For this division, time zone and location are not important, but it is key that employees and vendors are subject matter experts covering the area their clients work in. Other companies would prefer to structure them by process, for example, creating different teams of project managers, vendor managers, etc to work on all the tasks related to transcreation, translation, interpreting, etc.

As far as I know, all these structures can be equally efficient and often companies try different structures over time until they find a good balance that fits their needs. Divisions different to the ones mentioned here might also exist. This is probably why restructuring and re-arrangement of teams and roles is a normal occurrence for many companies every few years. In my experience, it is a great feeling of accomplishment seeing your company change their structure and evolve over time. It is a must that companies adapt to the changes and demands of the market, restructuring teams and scaling when needed. Although, sometimes, these transitions are not smooth for employees and it can take some time to adapt to new procedures. This happens often when a company is growing.

I have worked in teams divided by client/industry, and by language, and I find both options viable. Small teams working with the same client and projects tend to understand more of the big picture and adapt their own personal way of working to their teammates to achieve the same goal. Bigger teams need stronger coordination via their team leads to ensure everyone understands each other's roles, and keeps in mind the big picture while working to achieve the same goal. In the end, the work we do through our companies helps develop the world, and it is only fair that we keep up with the changes.

Chapter 2
Pool Equipment:
The Vendor Management Role

2.1. Job Responsibilities

The basic responsibilities of a member of the vendor management team are always the same few:

- → database management,
- → recruitment and onboarding of new vendors,
- → support of other teams within the company,
- → management and monitoring of vendors,
- → reporting.

Depending on the needs of the company, the vendor management team might have additional core responsibilities such as quality management, or processing vendors' invoices.

It is important to notice that working hours aren't evenly split among these job responsibilities as the prioritisation of some tasks over others depends on the company's objectives and procedures. If the company is growing their client base, the team might spend most of their time recruiting proactively to ensure a steady team of vendors for future demands. On the other hand, if the company is consolidating and going through a period of little change, the team might spend more time on database management such as clean-up, data transfer, process improvement, etc.

When I started working as a vendor manager, I had been a project coordinator for about two years. My expectation was that this role would work in a similar fashion: work on a set of projects per month with a start date and deadline, while saving some ongoing admin tasks to do during less hectic days. Because of this mindset, I used to get frustrated and felt burnt-out during busier periods. I didn't see the positive impact of my daily effort managing vendors on the overall company, as I was just focused on the day-to-day work.

It took me about three years to realise that vendor management doesn't work the same way as project management. The tasks we perform don't usually have a set start date or deadline and they are always needed, so long as the company is active. Therefore, there will always be a need to recruit vendors, update different profiles in the database, send feedback, manage vendors, etc.

Because of this way of working, it is important for us to see the big picture and monitor how the company changes over time thanks to our regular achievements. I will talk about this more in detail in the next chapter.

Database Management

A vendor management team will be in charge of maintaining the database and do periodical clean-ups to make sure data is relevant and accurate for the rest of the company. This includes actions such as recording vendors' availability, keeping each profile up-to-date, and ensuring new information is recorded for future reference. The team needs to collect all documents and relevant information from all vendors as well as ensure they adhere to contract and confidentiality terms. They will also communicate with them regularly as their first point of contact for queries and feedback.

Monitoring Performance

A vendor management team is responsible for monitoring the vendors' performance regularly. They gather information by communicating with the relevant internal teams to ensure feedback is sent to the vendors regarding their performance. Moreover, they work with other teams within the company and vendors to improve future performance. If vendors don't meet the company's standards of quality or service, the vendor management team is responsible for their off-boarding and removal from the database.

I believe vendors are more often removed because of their incompatibility with the company's way of working and processes rather than because of quality related issues. This highlights the importance of monitoring behaviour of vendors as much as the quality of their work. Afterall, the collaboration between company and vendor is a business relationship between humans, with different personalities and standards that are not entirely objective. Since I began my new role six months ago, 70% of the vendors I have removed from the database were due to behaviour issues such as late deliveries, rejection of feedback, communication issues and lack of availability.

Engagement of Vendors

Keeping vendors engaged is one of the trickiest parts of being a vendor manager. It's partly because of the bias against LSPs I mentioned before, as well as the erratic nature of the work as it is not always possible to ensure a regular stream of work to every vendor in the database. If you were a vendor working for your company, how would you like them to engage with you?

It requires a bit of creativity and a lot of time and empathy. Unfortunately, many companies don't think of it as a top priority, but in my opinion, this is one of the core responsibilities for the vendor management team. It helps building and developing relationships with vendors and strengthens the cooperation of both sectors in the industry. Later in the book, I will talk about strategies that worked for me and what is trending in the industry. It always works best when these engagement actions are done according to the company's culture and budget, so vendors truly feel they have meaningful collaboration with the company.

Company Support

Another key responsibility is to support different teams within the company such as sales, quality and project management, recommending vendors and influencing the usage of certain vendors over others through vendor promotion. The cooperation between these teams impacts recruitment and onboarding of new vendors when needed as well as off-boarding. Because of the vendor management team's deep knowledge of the company's pool of vendors, many teams and executive management require their input and advice on projects and company-wide decisions regularly.

Reporting and Other Administrative Tasks

A vendor management team creates reports periodically for the rest of the company, sharing any changes or significant updates related to the vendor pool. These reports are usually related to their key performance indicators (KPIs), which I have added to the end of this chapter and are tied to the functions of the software available to the team. A primary task of a vendor management team is to monitor buying rates and costs related to testing, as this will help the company manage their spend.

If all this wasn't enough to keep the team busy, a vendor management team also invests some time in improving existing processes by analysing trends within the vendor pool as well as the company's internal teams. These improvements can be anything from introducing a new piece of software to changing the onboarding process, reducing the time it takes to onboard a new vendor. They help the company be more efficient overall.

2.2. Daily Work and Tasks

Email, instant message communication platforms and phone systems are a vendor management team's best daily ally, both to communicate with vendors and colleagues alike. Some companies also use tracking software to better organise the company's internal communication and avoid sending too many emails.

It is also important to note that the vendor management team often works with the vendors' database which usually is part of the business management system (Plunet, XTRF, etc.).

As mentioned before, the vendor management team's main responsibilities of recruiting, database management, and supporting other teams are large, continuous tasks that involve short term actions. Recruitment is done as per the company's needs of new vendors; therefore, it is an activity that will be ongoing throughout the year. For example, in January you could be looking for German into English translators for marketing and in May you may be asked to recruit English into French medical vendors.

The same goes for database management, as these responsibilities involve communicating with vendors regarding changes in the company, performance meetings, or even a larger task like a database clean-up. We will explore these in detail in the next chapter. On the other hand, reporting is only done a limited number of times during the year, for example monthly, quarterly or yearly.

However, when a vendor management team works on a task directly supporting other teams within the company, they will be limited by deadlines ranging from a couple of hours to a couple of months or longer. A short-term example is providing vendor recommendations for an urgent job or long term, such as having to prepare a pool of vendors for different language combinations for a new client.

A good vendor management team needs to be able to juggle several ongoing tasks at the same time, so to ensure we don't lose sight of the bigger picture. I recommend creating a timeline from 3 months to 1 year, where the team adds all the long-term and short-term tasks assigned to them. I use it as a holistic to-do list, where deadlines, phases and tasks are added to give a comprehensive picture of the work the team is carrying out. This tool will help the team stay on top of their work as well as manage their capacity and productivity. It can also be linked to each team member's key performance indicators and objectives.

I believe that vendor management is a complex and dynamic function. Although it can be very administrative at times, it allows you to interact with people all over the world on a regular basis, which is what I most enjoy about this role.

At the start of the day, the inbox is full of different requests from vendors. Some may need help with invoicing, access to the vendor portal or send you an availability update; others will send their CVs to be considered for future collaboration. Most of the day will be spent sending emails. Apart from answering queries, you might need to send entry tests to new candidates and send files for revision. These are usually what are considered priority tasks, as it has to do with vendor management and support to other teams within the company.

Because vendor management is a core function within the business, the team will need to attend meetings with colleagues to talk about recruitment needs, availability of vendors or issues happening in live projects.

I usually leave all administrative tasks for the afternoon, after the much-needed lunch break. These tasks are not usually considered priority and include creating reports for executive management, updating information in the database, checking all documentation is in the right folders, creating and removing profiles from the database, etc.

Most vendor managers I know work alone or in small teams of two, so it can get a bit stressful at times. Sometimes, it seems like there are many vendors to take care of on top of answering your colleagues' requests. Therefore, focusing on the bigger picture with tasks such as having a daily to-do list, a short-term plan and a few long-term objectives, can help you rise above water, instead of drowning under everyday requests.

2.3. Skillset

I believe all of us should have a job we are able to enjoy. After all, we spend about 8 hours per day doing it. If you don't enjoy interacting with different people throughout the day, working on several tasks at the same time or being in a fast-paced environment, this is probably not the role for you. Anyone can train to be a successful member of a vendor management team and probably any other roles out there. However, daily work will be more enjoyable if some of the skills I mention below come naturally to you or you are keen to develop over time.

Back in 2020, I surveyed some of my peers on LinkedIn to come up with a list of the most important skills they search for in a vendor management team member. Company owners, other vendor managers and even project managers participated. The answers were very interesting as all of them ranked these skills differently and prioritised them according to the needs of their company at the time.

For example, some people highlighted good communication skills, because their company's goal was to improve their vendors' engagement with the company; others thought it was more important to be able to come up with outside-the-box ideas to recruit new vendors as they were looking to increase their pool. Therefore, it is important to note that this is not an exhaustive list and I have only added to this section the basic skills we agreed upon at the time. After further research, I also noticed that these basic skills are present in most job descriptions when looking for a vendor management role and I would suggest adding them to your curriculum. This increases the chances of your profile being picked up by any recruiter searching for new talent.

The skills below are key to be able to perform any vendor management role successfully:

- Excellent communication skills
- Ability to develop and maintain strong and successful working relationships
- Industry awareness
- Numeracy skills
- A flair for negotiation and networking
- Making important decisions and coping with the pressure of demanding targets and tight deadlines

Excellent Communication Skills

Any vendor management team needs to communicate with different people daily: teammates, colleagues, vendors, and sometimes, clients. Managing the database gives the team a lot of knowledge about the company's vendors, its strengths and weaknesses, so they are the best people to answer their colleagues' questions. A good example of this is when the sales team asks if the company can provide an unusual language combination or when the project management team enquires about the availability of certain vendors over a holiday period, etc.

A good vendor management team also needs to be able to attract suitable vendors to work with the company, provide written and oral feedback in a tactful manner and interact with people from different countries. It is crucial that the team is aware of personality types and the ways people communicate in different cultural backgrounds to be able to avoid and resolve misunderstandings. For example, a colleague told me that a vendor asked to be removed from the database of a company because the project manager didn't write *Hello* or *How are you?* in their email communication with this vendor. This was misunderstood as a rude and inappropriate gesture during a business conversation in the vendor's home country.

Ability to Develop and Maintain Strong and Successful Working Relationships

One of a vendor management team's core responsibilities is to be able to create and develop business relationships with the company's vendors, as well as maintain and improve them during their collaboration. Engagement tactics and long-term plans are developed and used by companies to develop a good working relationship with their vendors. Sporadic phone calls, business review meetings, newsletters, feedback discussions are all used effectively.

A few years ago, after working regularly with the same vendors for several months, I arranged for Christmas cards and chocolates to be sent to them on behalf of the company as a gesture of appreciation of our business relationship. Their response was very positive, as they felt appreciated and valuable to the company, strengthening the business relationship we already had. This had many benefits, including making them available to work with us more often.

Industry Awareness

A vendor management team needs to be aware of how the industry operates in every country to recruit efficiently and provide their best work. This can save the company a lot of money and time on vendor recruitment and relationship management.

Nowadays, I think it is a must for any employee to attend industry events, read industry articles, network with peers, etc. but more so, for a vendor management team. Resources currently available in Women in Localization, GALA, ELIA and other associations are priceless. However, some of the knowledge has been moved to social media and following the right people can fill your feed with interesting information every minute.

There were a couple of times over the years where I have had to answer questions from different clients regarding the variant of Chinese language they should use for their content. After doing some research, I was able to put together an internal document with information on the different options available in the database and the market at the time and what was generally used in the industry that could be useful to sales representatives and project managers alike.

Numeracy Skills

This might seem like an odd skill for a vendor management team, because databases are built on vendor profiles, not numbers. However, most of the vendor management team's objectives are measured in numbers and percentages, for example, the number of translators recruited or removed from the database, the percentage of passed and failed tests, etc. It's why the team should be able to analyse and present this information clearly and accurately to their colleagues and the company's upper management. Currently, I am working on an analysis on the company's productivity rates as we work with several CAT tools and machine translation engines. It requires a lot of numbers and percentages to be thoroughly checked.

A Flair for Negotiation and Networking

A good vendor management team should always understand the main negotiation principles and be able to apply them, as well as know how to network successfully in a business environment. Avoiding negotiation and networking situations could result in losses for the company. This is also a useful skill to have when dealing with escalation management, as the vendor management team might need to work and be responsible for resolving conflict situations between the company and certain vendors. Only a handful of times in my career have I been involved in a situation where I have had to mediate between the company and a vendor when payment was refused or collaboration was suddenly stopped. It is a difficult situation to be in that requires empathy. It can become a complex matter to deal with and these skills can help achieve a smooth resolution of the matter.

Making Important Decisions and Coping with the Pressure of Demanding Targets and Tight Deadlines

Given that the database is one of the most valuable assets of a company, a vendor management team bears a big responsibility when managing and developing it to suit the company's needs and objectives. Sometimes the team is required to advise or make important decisions that widely affect the company. Some decisions are not easy to make and, added to the pressure of tight deadlines, the vendor management team needs to be ready to recruit vendors against the clock.

Here's an example. A client requests voiceover services for Navajo language. The team would need to research if there is any vendor available in the market that offers the service for this language and might advise the client to proceed with subtitling instead or reject the request altogether, offering an alternative solution to the client's needs.

There are two skills that didn't make it to the final list, maybe because they are the basis of any role in the Language Services Industry: good multitasking and time management. Both these can be learned with practice and there are several courses and books available to help you become a master of time and prioritisation. A special recommendation I would like to add here is *The 7 Habits of Highly Effective People*, written by Stephen R. Covey.

2.4. Vendor Management Team and Structure

Different variations on job titles you can have as a vendor management team member has been a hot topic in the Translation Vendor Management group I run on LinkedIn lately, so it seems right to mention it here.

We all have different names, depending on how the company considers their vendors and processes. For example, in industry jargon, the words talent, supplier, resource, provider, partner, are often used instead of vendor. Therefore, many colleagues have the job title of talent manager, partner relationship manager, resource manager, supplier manager, etc. This can also be reflected in the team's name as some companies call their vendor management function supply chain management, resource, sourcing or outsourcing, reflecting the value and expectations the company assigns their vendor management team and therefore their vendors.

During April 2022, I ran a survey among different vendors on LinkedIn asking them what they would like to call their role when working for a LSP. The poll was open for two weeks and 142 people responded. Results showed preferred names were linguist, vendor/provider/resource and partner, but only a handful of people chose talent. Some people commented that talent is often used in human resources instead of vendors, and to refer to employees, others mentioned that "vendor" implied a negative connotation, in their opinion.

Generally, among LSPs, it is believed that calling your vendors partners or talent, implies a level of closeness that the words supplier or provider doesn't achieve. I personally believe actions speak louder than words, so it all boils down to how you treat your vendors, not what you call them.

LSPs have the tendency to be quite secretive about their vendor management processes, as it is such a core function for the company. There are several ways that a vendor management team can be structured, and it depends on the company's goals and priorities. However, there are many similarities when it comes to the basics. In this section, I will mention the ones I have had the opportunity to experience during my professional career.

Generally, there are four tiers within a team, depending on the employee's experience and how big the team is. Starting from junior, coordinator or assistant vendor manager, then moving up to, vendor manager, followed by senior vendor manager and, finally, team lead or head of vendor management.

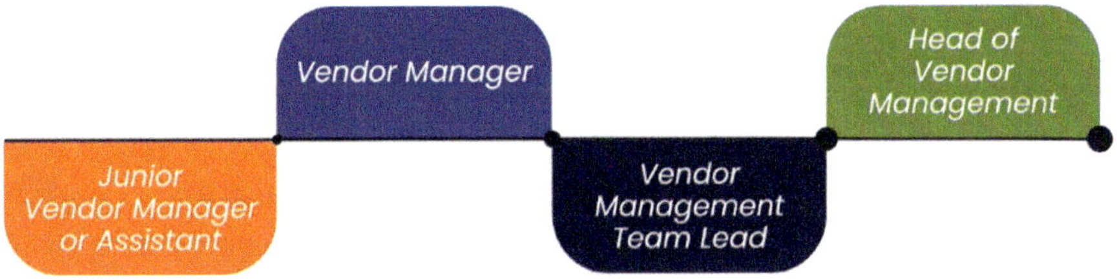

The most basic team structure happens in small and some medium size companies where there is only one person dedicated to vendor management. These are companies that haven't got many vendors and/or have been working with the same vendors for a long time, so the volume of work is manageable for a single person. The positives of being in this position is the amazing room for development and improvement the vendor manager has daily. However, it can become pretty stressful during busier periods. Most of my career I have been holding the fort as the only vendor manager of my company, so I am very familiar with the feeling of having too much to do and not enough time. When this happens, my advice is to add all the tasks and deadlines to a to-do list and communicate with your colleagues about which tasks have the highest priority.

On the next level are vendor management teams from two to four members, where there is a team lead and a couple of vendor co-ordinators and/or managers, depending on their years of experience in the role. This set-up usually happens in medium size companies where there is a great need for recruitment, supplier management and database clean-up. The team will share tasks evenly, so that everyone is aware of their teammates' workload and can cover and support when needed.

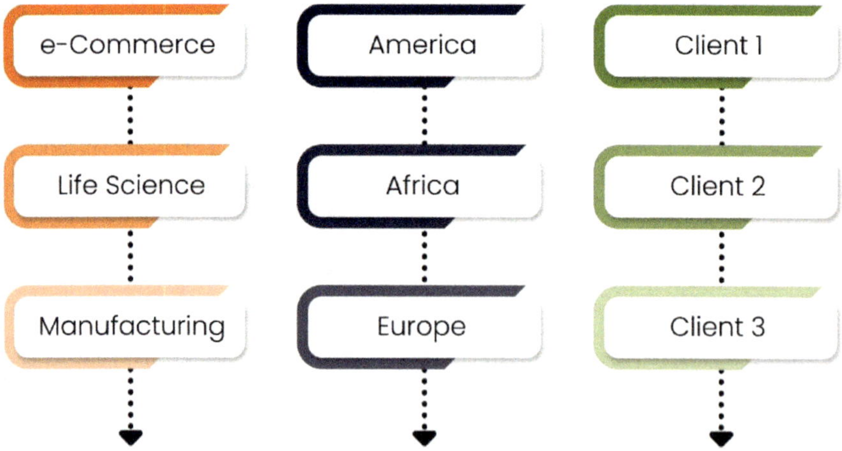

Bigger companies with a varied pool of vendors will usually employ 5 or more vendor managers and create a different structure according to their needs. These vendor management teams can be divided in different categories such as by language combination/region, client/

subject matter, or service. It can also happen that the job responsibilities are also split within the team so that each team member oversees performing or co-ordinating a different task, such as a recruitment specialist, an onboarding specialist, a trainer, etc.

The vendor management teams divided by language or region will ensure each team member takes charge of a set of vendors for certain language combinations or regions. This division can be as specific as the company needs, according to their vendors and workload. For example, a company offering translation services for most languages can divide their team per region such as Europe, the Middle East and Africa (EMEA), Asia-Pacific (APAC) languages, etc. However, a company offering interpreting services in Europe only, might prefer to divide their team according to Nordic languages, Balkan languages, etc.

If the company has a wide variety of clients requesting different subject matters for a small range of languages, the team might be more efficient when divided by client or subject matter. This means each teammate will take charge of a specific pool of dedicated vendors, manage their profiles and recruit new vendors when needed.

As an example, one or more team members will take care of all the ad-hoc clients and their sporadic requests, while another small team will look after a major client in the e-Commerce industry and their regular projects, then another teammate will co-ordinate the vendor management needs for a few smaller clients requesting regular legal translations. On the other hand, if the company offers several services, the vendor management team could be more effective when divided by service, making each member an expert in their field when it comes to recruitment, negotiation and general knowledge of the project cycle and best practices for each service.

As you might have guessed, recruitment for translation is different from recruiting voice over artists or formatting vendors, and the vendor management team needs a wider variety of experience to be able to carry out different types of recruitment successfully. For example, a company that gets translation, copywriting and formatting requests regularly from their clients would need a team of vendor managers with experience in recruiting each different vendor type. This means they need to be able to discern the expert vendors from vendors who are trying it out.

However, these different structures are not set in stone, and it might be that some companies would benefit from a mixture of these divisions to achieve their ultimate goal, without exhausting their team members and making sure all their vendors are managed. The team could be primarily divided by clients and be responsible for some specific languages or services, co-ordinating any vendor management action needed with their teammates when necessary. In my experience, each member of the vendor management team would be able to take care of around 200 vendors regularly active. This is a very subjective number as we would also need to consider the overall workload and responsibilities of the entire vendor management team.

Because of the way the industry is spread and the high amount of small and medium companies out there, it is likely that vendor managers work alone or in small teams. That is why networking is so important. It can get a bit lonely, and it is important to find colleagues who understand the little frustrations and joys of our daily work.

In 2021, I did some consulting and training 1:1 for other vendor managers and I remember them being surprised at how good it felt to share their experiences with me and get some useful tips about the work.

2.5. Vendor Management Manual

Having a vendor management manual is key to the success of a team. It is important for all team members to have a file as a point of reference where the role is explained and information is laid out in a very detailed manner so it can be used as reference, as well as a guide for the training of newer employees. In my experience, most companies have some version of this kind of document, as it is required for ISO certifications and audits. However, is it as detailed as the vendor management team members need it to be? Here are some tips on how to build a vendor management manual that will provide the instructions and information your team needs to do their best work.

Consider this, does your current manual mention where the credentials for recruitment platforms are stored? Is the team aware of the official process to follow when adding a new vendor to the database? What about KPIs? Does the team know the information they need to add on their reports?

A vendor management manual will gather all the processes related to vendor management: standard operating procedures, rules of thumb, etc. It would also contain the company's expectations towards the team members and how the team fits in the company's structure.

Start by explaining the company's approach to their vendors and clients. What is the general company guideline when it comes to what is expected from them and the mutual collaboration? Then, move on to the company's expectations and hopes for the vendor management team specifically. Explain how they fit in the company structure and their relation to all the other teams.

Define the role's responsibilities and team structure. This section might change over time as the company develops and team changes, so it is important that it becomes a live document which is updated regularly.

It also connects to the next section where you can include company processes and how to carry out the team's responsibilities mentioned earlier. Be as detailed as possible, so the team can follow them without additional support: add links, screenshot images and specific steps.

This is the part of the manual that team members will re-read most often and it is also expected to change as technology and processes are updated. To close this section, describe the vendor management team's key performance indicators (KPIs). For example, answer the following questions: What areas of the vendor management team will you monitor to measure the team's success? How often?

The next section can contain tips, specific advice taken from experience, maybe even industry resources that might come in handy when doing the job. Remember to add any shared credentials for platforms as well, specific bits of information that are helpful such as the payment breakdown the company uses, which CAT tools the company can provide, which services are usually required for each client, etc.

Going a step further, the vendor management manual doesn't have to be a boring black and white document full of bullet points and even paragraphs. Update it with a company logo and colour scheme, add pictures of team members and their hobbies, mention their individual responsibilities or general objectives. Why not add a section with the team's main achievements and update it on a regular basis?

Imagine the feeling of confidence having a vendor manual with all this information on your first day in a new vendor management role, along with this book. With both these tools, you will ensure training on your new role is smooth and quick, so you feel ready to start working.

2.6. Key Performance Indicators (KPIs) for Vendor Management

Key Performance Indicators are used to evaluate the success of an activity. In the context of the vendor management team, it refers to periodic achievements to a level of satisfaction, but also in terms of making progress toward a bigger goal. KPIs are guided by the company's priorities and goals for the vendor management team. There are several areas that can be measured when it comes to the team's responsibilities. The list shown below is not exhaustive given that it very much depends on the functionalities of the company's database platform and the data recorded on a regular basis by team members, but it is a very good starting point to use as reference.

Main Performance Indicators:

- Vendors onboarded
- Vendors offboarded
- Cost of testing
- Testing success rate

Additional Indicators:

- Demonstration of saving after rate negotiation
- Improvement of quality of deliverables after providing feedback
- Number of profiles updated in database
- New vendors usage
- Positive impact of the engagement of vendors
- Volume and type of support given to other teams within the company
- Reports on time spent on different tasks
- ime taken to onboard a new vendor
- Progress on specific admin tasks, i. e. recruitment, databases clean-up, process improvement, etc.

Chapter 3

Dipping Our Toes: Database Management

3.1. Managing the Database

A vendor database is a tool for internal teams to find the best vendors available for any given project. All the vendors' information will be in it and in many instances, it is connected to the management platform and billing software. Some of the current business management systems used in the industry are XTRF, Protemos, LBS Suite, Plunet, and many more. The way the information is organised across these platforms is very similar, at least for Plunet and XTRF, as those are the ones I have had the chance to use during my career.

The creation of a project management system integrated with a vendor database is the main recent advancement in automation for vendor management. More and more companies are adapting XTRF, Plunet, etc to manage their projects' and their vendors' information.

There is a search engine that allows you to filter the vendor you are looking for according to different categories such as language combination, location, specialisation, etc. Each vendor profile has several fields to be completed by them or the company like billing address, telephone number, rates, and so on. There is also a section to upload documents and a section to mark a vendor's availability. Some systems include a quality management section, where both internal employees and vendors can add feedback on the work performed by each vendor in their profile.

As we saw before, it is the vendor management team's duty to manage it strategically to maximise its usability and ensure it is flexible, and cost-effective. This means the cost of maintaining the vendor database must be small, vendors must be used as much as possible, and the variety of vendors must be flexible enough to cope with extraordinary requests or peaks in the workload.

No matter the size of the database, there is always a risk of data getting out of control. Unlike other industries, the database the vendor management team deals with, big or small, changes probably every week. Therefore, the team will be looking after the vendor database daily to keep it cohesive, updated and tidy. A database with outdated information or incomplete profiles is every company's worst nightmare. Tasks such as a full database clean-up, mass on-boarding and removal of vendors takes a lot of a vendor management team's time and effort. Hence, effective daily management of the database is the most beneficial in terms of cost and employee motivation.

Information on the database will be used by other teams, so it should be laid out in a user-friendly manner, and be accessible for the rest of the teams when necessary.

I like to write guidelines on how to add and edit information in the database, for example best practices when creating a new profile, updating the information on a profile, and when removing a profile. Also, these guidelines can help database users find the specific information they need. For example, characteristics that the vendor must meet in order to be removed from the database are: a lack of work in the last 18 months, bad feedback on the last three jobs, or email address or phone number not working.

I suggest organising training sessions with other teams in the company, so they feel confident and are self-sufficient when using the database, or if they have to modify information in any vendor's profile. This training is most important when new employees join the company. Because the database is used by different teams to contact vendors, parameters should be put in place so vendors are contacted objectively, for example categorising them in a way that they can be the most effective to the company. Use of the maximum number of vendors regularly is very important in ensuring that flexibility and quality of the database is maintained.

To go one step further, the key to a healthy database is to be able to know when vendors are available to work for the company. This will help a vendor management team identify gaps, such as periods where certain service or language combinations might be limited in supply. I advise starting with the most requested languages and services, and to be aware of any national or religious holiday periods. This information will help the rest of the company planning their workload, but also provide the vendor management team with information on any services or languages that need to be added to the recruitment plan.

I am so grateful that this part of the work has been improved thanks to automation, however, there is still a long way to go. After talking to my peers, many of us agree that current Business Management Systems (BMSs) could be improved to help automating vendor management administrative tasks even more, helping us focus on what is important and cannot be automated: building better relationships with vendors.

It's for this reason we are putting together an open letter through the LinkedIn group, Translation Vendor Management, directed to technology providers in the industry suggesting improvements to current systems as well as offering our expertise and knowledge as consultants and testers.

3.2. Database Clean-up

Cleaning the database can be a mammoth task which can make any vendor management team feel like scribes from the Middle-Ages. Let's pause for a moment and think about the questions below. Once you have answered these questions you can start creating your clean-up master plan.

What does your company need from the database?

What is the purpose of the database clean-up?

What is the current status of the database?

It is important to keep the main objective of the clean-up task in mind while drawing up all these actions, and to remember data in the database must be useful, effective, valid, accurate, complete, consistent and uniform across all profiles.

First, identify the issues to be solved, then, create a list of the actions that need to be taken by the team to rectify them. These actions need to be detailed enough so they are accurate as per the time they will take to complete. Also, mention if help from other departments might be needed, for example the quality team or the finances department.

Next, I suggest creating a timeline with all the different stages and assigning an estimated deadline for the completion of each step. If the database is bigger than a few hundred vendors, divide the profiles into smaller groups, for example by language, client, subject matter, on-boarding date, or even location.

Example:

<u>What is the purpose of the database clean-up?</u>

Database information to be complete and reliable.

<u>What is the current status of the database?</u>

60% of the profiles in the database are missing crucial information, such as telephone number or the vendors' CV.

<u>What does your company need from the database?</u>

Ensure all profiles are ISO compliant before the audit in May.

<u>Actions:</u>

- Identify non-ISO complaint profiles - 2 weeks
- Contact vendors to provide the missing information - 3 weeks

I estimate it would take a single vendor manager around eight months to finish the clean-up process for a database of 1000 vendors, taking into account this task would be combined with the rest of their daily job requirements.

As mentioned before, the task might need some input from other departments depending on how many different teams work with the information in the database. Communication with colleagues as well as upper management should be fluent and regular, so that everyone is up to date on the status of the clean-up tasks. I would advise to share the timeline and status with other employees during monthly company meetings, for example.

It is advisable to create or update guidelines in the vendor management manual for the processing of this data, that also mention the recording and managing of data in the future. This will help standardise information contained in the database and keep it in good order. If the clean-up involves a change of software or any structural change in the general vendor management process, making sure there is written documentation of the new procedures put in place after the clean-up is even more crucial. This ensures everyone will follow the same steps when adding or editing data on the database. This process should fit within company guidelines as well as take into account compliance with ISO and GDPR regulations.

The last action in your plan should be to add a clean-up follow-up date to ensure all information in the database is still accurate as time progresses. For example, planning an annual sanity check of the database where the profiles of newly recruited and regularly used vendors are checked.

Follow these simple, but effective steps and I am certain these guidelines will make you feel like a master organiser. Not only that, but they will help you take ownership of the tedious task of cleaning up the database, giving you a sense of achievement and pride.

I performed my last database clean-up a few months ago, when I arrived at Ultimate Languages. The PMs were only using part of the database and there were many vendors who hadn't been contacted in a few months or didn't have any information in their profiles. As a newcomer to the company, I didn't have any background information on their performance or their history of work with Ultimate Languages, so that made my job much harder. I contacted all the vendors in the database several times, and little by little, I cleared up the clutter, updating every profile. Nowadays, the database looks a bit smaller, but it is much more effective and user friendly. PMs use a wider range of vendors and can easily find all the necessary information in each profile. It was a bit discouraging at times, but I knew I was investing my time in something beneficial for everyone in the company, and now that is done, maintenance is much more straightforward. I have achieved my main objective of the year.

Chapter 4

Jumping in:

Vendor Recruitment

4.1. Recruiting

Recruitment is one of the main responsibilities of a vendor management team. Companies highlight this task in any vendor management job description, and because it is easy to measure, it is part of the key performance indicators of the team. Given that recruitment is such an important part of the vendor management role, companies create and follow recruitment plans to be able to find and onboard the most suitable vendors in the least possible time. It usually starts when a need for new vendors is identified by any team in the company. For example, when the sales team acquires a new client, or the project management team has to deal with a new language combination.

In my experience, recruitment can be proactive or reactive. Proactive means the vendor management team analyses trends in workload and the status of the database and recruits, regularly anticipating any needs the company might have in the future. A reactive approach is when the vendor management team recruits new vendors as requests come in, often in a rush. This method, although effective, can be overwhelming and create a burn-out feeling within the team. However, recruiting proactively for future needs can lead to a waste of money and time for the company, as projections might not materialise.

I recommend maintaining a balance between the two approaches in a way that fits between the clients' requests and the teams' capacity, creating a vendor strategy that keeps the database flexible in periods of high and low demand. This means using vendors in a strategic manner to achieve company goals while minimising the risk of overspending on testing tasks.

Your vendor management team will need the following information before contacting potential vendors:

- Language combination ______________________________
- Client's name ______________________________
- Subject area / content ______________________________
- Tasks (translation, revision, post-editing, etc) ________________
- Estimated volume and regularity ______________________________
- Budget per unit (source words, hour, minute, etc.) ______________
- CAT tool ______________________________
- Number of vendors required ______________________________
- Sample of content to use as test (optional) ________________
- Background information on the task - workflow ______________
- Vendor Management deadline ______________________________

A recruitment plan can take from one week to two months or more, depending on the language combination and subject matter. Sometimes, recruiting involves a lot of searching, other times, the vendor management team spends longer in building a relationship with potential new vendors. Once the task has been completed, the team can analyse the results and learn from the work carried out in retrospect.

The vendor management team searches the internet for professional vendors that match the project's requirements - from translators and interpreters, to copywriters, voiceover artists, formatters, accessibility professionals, transcreators and even other LSPs. For every step involved in the project life cycle, the vendor management team will need to find a vendor that can provide the service or services needed. A very simplified and general example is a project where the company needs to localise a video from English into Spanish. The vendor manager would need to find, at least, an English transcriber, a Spanish translator, a Spanish voice over artist and an audio engineer.

Currently, most used platforms for recruitment are Proz.com, LinkedIn and all the different translation associations' web pages such as ATA, ITI, AUSIT, etc. Most countries have their own translators and interpreters' associations. Sometimes it is useful if you are looking for vendors located in a specific country. There are also associations created by companies such as GALA, ELIA and ATC, to name a few. However, it is important to mention that not all vendors out there belong to an association or have a consistent presence online. It also depends on the service these vendors offer. You can find out about any kind of service provider on LinkedIn, but there are other websites where vendors advertise themselves, such as Freelanly, Fiverr, PeoplePerHour, Zing, Voices, etc. Some directories have got a search engine where you can add the language combination you are looking for as well as specialism. This makes our search much easier.

Recruiting for languages with few native speakers can be a difficult task sometimes. I always recommend reaching out to governmental bodies, non-profit organisations, language schools, universities, etc. as they might be able to recommend potential vendors or reach out to them on your behalf.

Receiving referrals from other vendors and industry peers is a very trustworthy way to get good leads on potential vendors to add to the company's database. Companies used to be much more secretive about the vendors they use than they are now. So much so, that some companies refuse to provide recommendations or reviews publicly (as a letter or on social media). I don't agree with this approach and much prefer companies that are proud of their vendors and provide public recommendations, even to the point of featuring on their website or pitching to their client.

A different way to recruit new vendors is to save and monitor the big number of spontaneous applications that appear in the vendor management team's inboxes every day. It may be a bit riskier given that some of those CVs might be from scammers, but it is worth considering when an application seems professional and trustworthy. If these applications are saved, organised and filtered correctly, it can save a team several hours of searching.

Scammers are a big thing in our industry as there are a lot of people working freelance. They pretend to be a client or a vendor and attract unaware victims with promises of money. There isn't a rule of thumb that can help you discern whether a vendor is real or fake, so I suggest applying common sense and following your instinct.

4.1.1. General Recruitment Process

Most vendor management teams will recruit vendors by posting adverts on social media or other platforms and contacting vendors one by one through their profiles and websites. Therefore, being able to craft an attractive advert and introductory email is key to gain the interest and trust of the vendors you contact - your leads.

In my opinion, this isn't a one-size-fits-all. The content should be adapted to match the company's culture, but also the culture of the vendors you are recruiting. No one likes to read through very long sentences, so keep in mind any character limits applicable and the length and formatting of your advert and introductory email.

Any advert and email should at least contain these sections:

- Quick introduction about you and the company.
- What are you looking for?
- What does the company offer?
- A bit of information on the company's onboarding process and next steps.
- What information do you need from the vendor?

Tips:

- Include the name of the recipient, if known.
- Mention your location or time zone, working hours.
- Use respectful and friendly language, while remaining clear and concise.

Vendors will probably do some research on the company and person sending the email before answering back, so having a consistent online presence is important, as well as being aware of the company's reviews on websites such as the Proz.com Blue Board and Glassdoor.

It is also common for a vendor to ask additional questions before agreeing to go through the onboarding process, such as payment terms, specific contract clauses or general details of the company's workflow. Therefore, it is essential for the vendor management team to be aware of general procedures and policies of the company, contract specifications and financial processes, to be able to answer these questions as swiftly as possible. If the recruitment process takes too long or is very complicated, the vendor might feel overwhelmed and disengage halfway through.

Some companies include a short interview or chat with the vendor and the filling of forms before proceeding with the onboarding process to see if a mutually beneficial collaboration would be possible before the next step of the process. This is a great way to get to know the vendor better and ensure they are what the company needs. However, given that the Language services industry is deadline-driven, some teams are under a lot of pressure to achieve the company's demand of vendors with very little time, so it is not always possible to follow best practices to the letter in every situation. The vendor management team and its procedures should be flexible, adapting the recruitment process according to each situation, when necessary, always keeping in mind any potential risks.

The most difficult job I had to recruit for was increasing the pool of vendors for an ongoing project involving small tasks with quick turnaround times for multiple languages. The client brief we were given was very specific and strict in terms of location, availability and price. Moreover, there were more than 15 different languages to be translated into and out of English. It was a time-consuming and never-ending task, as there were changes in the pool of vendors almost every week, some coming in and some leaving. Clearly, standard processes were not working, so we created and implemented a new process specific for this client, from specific wording on the contact email for now vendors to quality procedures and pricing strategy for each small job. With continuous monitoring and clear communication among the team, the pool stopped having such a continuous turnover and recruiting for this project became less daunting and difficult. Vendors became more available for the tasks, quality increased overall and the client was much more satisfied with our service than before.

4.2. Vendor Selection

Selecting the right vendor can be tricky if the vendor management team is not sure of the kind of profile they need. I have created a list of questions below to help clarify the team's criteria to use when selecting vendors. It works best together with any company guidelines and requirements from other internal teams:

What to look for in a CV?

Overall:

- Are there any spelling, grammar, or syntactic errors?
- Does it contain all the information you need?
- What does it tell you about their personality and way of working?

Personal details:

- Take note of the vendor's location and working hours.
- Source and target languages are clearly displayed.

Education:

- Countries of formal education match the vendor's language combinations.
- Certifications match your requirements.
- Does the vendor engage in continuous personal development (CPD)?

Expertise:

- Main subject matters of specialisation, if any.
- Description of previous clients/projects.
- CAT tools.
- What will be their standard productivity and general availability for your company?

When dealing with other LSPs, the selection process will be different as they don't always provide blind CVs for the vendor management team to evaluate.

- Is the vendor ISO certified?
- Number of employees and office locations.
- Database size.
- Has the vendor got any in-house linguists?
- Working hours and time zone coverage.
- Will the vendor provide a dedicated account manager or project manager for your requests?
- How does the vendor deal with customer complaints?
- A general overview of the vendor's recruitment and onboarding process.
- How does the vendor monitor the quality delivered to their customers?
- Ask for references from other customers or proven records.

There are some additional factors to consider when recruiting and selecting new vendors such as location (if differs from their original country), previous experience, and obviously, culture. During my experience, I have found that American-based vendors generally prefer phone calls and meetings during the recruitment process instead of just email communication, while Nordic vendors might prefer straightforward and clear conversations, sometimes even 1-line emails to long paragraphs. These examples are quite general and may not always be accurate. As you communicate with each specific vendor, you will start creating an idea of their personality and way of working.

Chapter 5

Diving Deep: Vendor Onboarding

5.1. Onboarding

Onboarding is the process a company follows from the selection phase until the vendor is ready to work with the company on live projects. This process might include testing, paperwork signing, training and even giving them access to different systems and software.

This is mainly done by the vendor management team, however, depending on the size of the company, the onboarding can be done by various teams, according to their competency. For example, the quality team might interact with the new vendor when it comes to quality standards and expectations, the project management team might support them with access to CAT tools or company specific training.

Sometimes we refer to onboarding when a vendor that is already in the database is added to a new client pool. To be added to this specific pool, they would need to complete a short onboarding step that can involve testing, training and being given access to the client's specific materials and tools. This is particularly useful to mitigate quality risks when working with a new client. It helps vendors familiarise themselves with the style and process that will be followed during live projects as well as give the vendor management team data on the amount of learning needed for each vendor to meet the client's expectations.

5.2. Testing

Testing is a default process in the localization industry for better or for worse. It consists of sending the vendor a short entry test, usually 200 to 300 words approximately. This task will have a strict deadline, as it also tracks the vendor's responsiveness and availability.

The entry test, or sample of work, is usually designed according to the work and specialism the vendor is going to perform in the future for a company and according to the language combination that the vendor masters. This entry test is assessed by a trusted vendor in the database or already included in the client pool, with the help of a quality matrix.

Unless the company has a software to measure quality, it is usually done in an Excel file. This document contains a formula that converts different error categories into a pass or fail score. These error categories are a mix of different quality models available in the market, but most of the ones I have worked with are based on the LISA quality model including terminology, mistranslation, etc.

The success of this entry test is the main factor a vendor management team will use when accepting a new vendor in the pool. Quality metrics can be very different depending on the criteria assessed and the software used.

As I have mainly worked with written translation projects and quality metrics during my career, I want to highlight the main points I consider a must have for any translation quality matrix.

In my opinion, any quality metric must take into account the number of words that are being checked, as it is not the same to have a result showing 4 errors in 300 words, rather than 3,000 words.

The quality matrix should also contain an area to provide the vendor with some positive feedback about their work.

As there is not a uniform matrix used across the industry, the document must contain detailed instructions of what needs to be evaluated and how. The lack of these instructions complicates the reviser's work and can render the revision as null, creating internal extra costs for the company.

The reviser is required to provide thorough objective evaluation of the choices made by the vendor when transferring the source into the target content. It is also important to ask the reviser to give their opinion on the style of the text, as for some clients/industries, it is a key component of what is considered good-quality work.

I want to point out that the quality matrix used to evaluate an entry test should be different to the matrix used to evaluate a live job. This is because the aim of the evaluation is completely different in both situations, in the same way two different services should have their own evaluation criteria.

In an entry test, the team is evaluating if a selected vendor is a good fit for future jobs requested by the company. However, a continuous check on the quality of live projects is designed to be swift, not to affect the deadline of the project, and to note and implement any errors that might have escaped the vendor's final check before delivery of the job to the client.

Last step of the testing process is providing the vendor with feedback, even when it is not positive. It might seem a bit uncomfortable to tell someone their work was not good enough after all the time and effort both parties have invested in the testing phase, but it is important for the vendor to have the result with examples they can analyse and learn from. This also gives the vendor management team a chance to see the vendors' reaction to feedback. Sometimes, it is best practice to ask for a third-party opinion if the vendor and reviser don't agree on the result.

5.3. Paperwork

In January 2022, I hosted an event for Women in Localization UK and there was a question from the audience that struck a chord.

It was related to the fact that the vendor management team spends an important amount of time dealing with paperwork: sending contracts for the vendors to sign, then perhaps a non-disclosure agreement, together with a form to fill in their details and services, and sometimes even some governmental tax forms to complete, when necessary, etc. Depending on the law in the country the company is based, printed records of these documents might be necessary as well.

All the information on these Word and PDF documents needs to be manually entered by someone into the database and other systems, for example a billing software. The team responsible for this task is none other than the vendor management team.

The introduction of Business Management Systems (BMSs) has improved this part of the work since I started my career, but this has remained pretty much unchanged. The platforms include a vendor portal, which is a feature where vendors can log in and update their details or claim or reject projects and invoice, however, these systems let the vendor management team vet this information so that nothing can be changed without our approval.

Of course, it largely depends on the company as some can afford tools that help with things such as electronic signing, where vendors can sign the company's contract effortlessly.

If the company is ISO certified, this is even more important as all the relevant information must be saved uniformly across the database for the auditor to verify once a year.

I can probably guess what you are thinking. Collecting, auditing and adding documents one by one to the database is demoralising when it is done repetitively for hundreds of different vendors. Luckily, we get faster and better at it with practise, so much so that there will come a day when your hands move along seamlessly out of muscle memory. Then, this task will take you two minutes instead of ten, and you can move on to more entertaining parts of the role.

5.4. Training

One of the latest steps in any basic onboarding process is training of the selected vendor. As we have seen, not all companies in the language services industry follow exactly the same procedures and use the same tools, so the vendor has to be trained on the specific procedures of the company as well as be aware of what is expected from them.

Some companies create a space where vendors can have a Frequently Asked Questions (FAQ) area with answers to their usual queries, such as payment terms, how to invoice their work, how they will be contacted when there is a new project, how to let the company know when they are unavailable, for example.

In terms of technical training, nowadays, most vendors are familiar with more than one tool, even if they do not own it, as it is a common industry practice to supply licences for specific tools, mostly CAT tools, to vendors during their work on a project, although vendors often buy their own CAT tool licences too. In addition to all the information available online in the shape of webinars, there are YouTube videos with instructions and online help manuals.

The training step is usually done through on demand video training, live meetings or providing the vendor with documents for them to read at their own pace. I think interactive ways of training will work best in most cases, but smaller companies might not be able to invest in such technology, pursuing other routes, such as providing the training materials in PPT and PDF format.

My advice would be to use it as a showcase for vendors to meet the internal team, promote the company's brand and encourage them to become an intrinsic part of the business. Of course, training is not just a one-off task, and some vendors might need a couple of months and several projects to be entirely familiar with the way the company works and what is expected from them.

Because I have worked in many small companies, I was only able to see and experience this part of the job at Akorbi in 2021. Their training system is complete with detailed information and updated regularly. It teaches vendors best practice when it comes to work with Akorbi as well as technical training and a repository to find all the information they might need in the future. In practice, some vendors hated it, some loved it. I thought it was a great system and wished smaller companies invested the time and resources into creating similar platforms.

5.5. Negotiation

First, let's consider the terms negotiation and power, which will be mentioned a lot moving forward. A business negotiation is a process where two parties aim to discover a common ground while holding their own aims, needs, and viewpoints. Power is important in negotiation because it helps influence one party over another.

Before diving deeper into the topic, I would like to highlight that negotiation is not always a must. Other methods of achieving the same outcome include using competitive bidding, persuasion, enforcement, problem-solving techniques and even directly complying with the vendor's demands. Depending on the situation, one of these techniques may be a better fit for solving a disagreement between the company and the vendor rather than using negotiation.

To make it as pragmatic as possible, I have divided the negotiation process into 3 steps: pre-negotiation, negotiation and post-negotiation phase.

5.5.1. Pre-negotiation Phase

This phase is also called the planning stage. It refers to the time spent in preparing before the negotiation takes place. It may not be the most exciting part of the process, but it is probably the most important as it can make the difference between success or failure of the negotiation.

This phase involves gathering data about the vendor, analysing the power each party has during the negotiation, identifying key objectives and priorities for the negotiation, and planning any tactics or strategies you may want to follow. To make it simple, I have created three categories inside this phase: gathering data, relationships and planning.

If the negotiation is going to take place during a meeting, or there is more than one person from each party involved, then it is important to align positions with them and prepare the meeting's agenda. However, most vendor management negotiations happen via email and telephone nowadays.

PRE-NEGOTIATION PHASE

- GATHERING DATA
- THE RELATIONSHIP
- PLANNING

The first step, gathering data, refers to finding out as much as you can about the vendor.

Try to answer the following questions about the vendor:

- How long has this vendor been collaborating with the company?
- Is this their first negotiation with the company?
- Were previous negotiations with this vendor successful?
- What is this vendor's performance like?
- What do the project managers say about this vendor?
- What is the market rate for this vendor's service and expertise?

Sometimes, this information would be easily found in the vendor's profile on the database, but often, project managers and/or in-house translators are a very good source of information when it comes to vendors. They may recall previous interactions with the vendor that the team may not be familiar with.

The second step of the pre-negotiation phase would be to analyse the company's relationship with the vendor. This relationship will greatly influence the negotiation. The aim is to determine how important this vendor is for the company, looking at the relationship through different filters.

One way of doing it is using this Power-Interest matrix. Dividing the company's vendors into four sections will help analyse the status of the database, according to their interest and negotiation power over the company.

High negotiation power, highly interested vendors (Manage Closely) should be engaged regularly, and the company should make the greatest efforts to satisfy them. These are key vendors, the ones the company works with almost daily and doesn't want to lose.

High negotiation power, less interested vendors (Keep Satisfied). Enough work should be put in to keep them satisfied, but not so much that they become displeased. These are the vendors you would beg to work on your projects.

Low negotiation power, highly interested vendors (Keep Informed) should be informed to ensure that they don't become disinterested. The vendors in this category offer a service or a language combination easy to resource and would be always happy to help in emergencies.

Low negotiation power, less interested vendor (Monitor). These are the vendors that are not needed often by the company and are happy with a transactional relationship only.

If looking at the relationship, you find that the company is dependent on the vendor's skills and availability to satisfy their clients, you won't possess a lot of power to control the business relationship, or any negotiation carried out with the vendor. You will have the upper hand during the negotiation, however, when you possess more power than the vendor in the relationship.

When planning a negotiation, the first decision to make is the approach. There are three main types of negotiation, according to the aim: seeking a win-lose outcome, accepting a lose-win outcome, or achieving a win-win outcome. Our industry usually exercises the win-win outcome approach. This is when both parties achieve their objectives, making the negotiation a success. This is the type of negotiation that will ensure a long-lasting relationship with the vendor, therefore it needs a high level of trust and openness, as well as flexibility from both parties.

Second, decide what you would like to achieve from the negotiation. I use Gavin Kennedy's LIM-it model which includes "must achieve" objectives, considered as deal-breakers; "intend to achieve" objectives, things that would be nice to accomplish; and "would like to achieve" objectives, the icing on the cake.

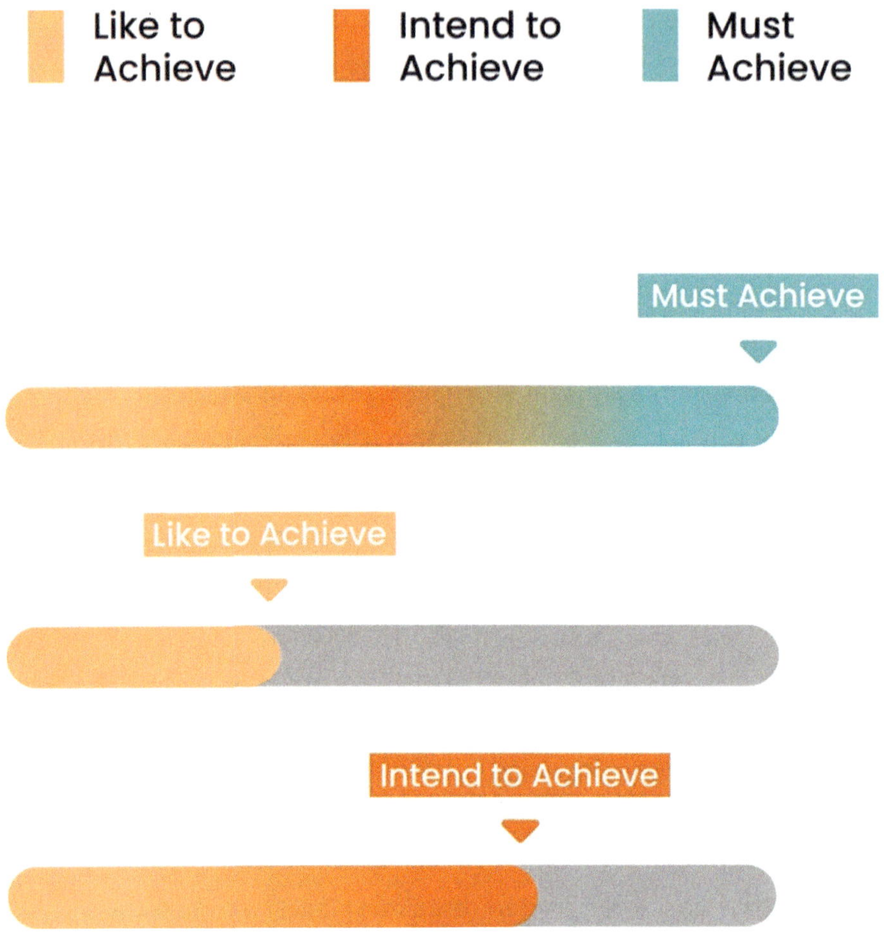

For example: during a negotiation with a vendor regarding hourly rates, the "must achieve" would be a rate equal to or lower than EUR 40 per hour, the "intend to achieve" would be a rate of EUR 38 per hour and the "would like to achieve" would be EUR 35 per hour.

Preparing this beforehand helps the team realise that if the vendor asks for EUR 35 per hour or more, one's bargaining power will need to be increased or they could decide to walk away from the negotiation. To avoid being caught in such a situation, it is wise to prepare predictions about the vendor's position and approach during the negotiation. This will help planning moves to counteract their actions.

Here are a few examples of how to increase bargaining power before a negotiation: appeal to market data or an expert's opinion in order to increase the credibility and value of your offer, and challenge the other party's position during the negotiation; preparing different tradeable items that can be brought to the table and used to one's advantage, such as money, time, support, flexibility etc; justifying the offer by appealing to forces beyond their control, i. e. "I am afraid our corporate policies wouldn't allow that"; ensuring that the company is an attractive customer to the vendor; or using influencing techniques which we will see later in the book.

It is important to also consider the different risks that involves negotiating with a vendor, for example, making unacceptable concessions giving them something the company cannot deliver on, not being able to reach an acceptable solution, damaging the relationship with the vendor, using conflicting tactics that compromise the position during a negotiation, as well as risks regarding the company's reputation, and legal risks.

To mitigate these risks, it is necessary that everything is prepared and planned so you can always counteract a vendor's moves during the negotiation phase.

5.5.2. Negotiation Phase

I have divided the negotiation phase into three stages: the opening, where you introduce the topic to the vendor, persuasion, which is the actual negotiation, and agreement and review, that refer to the conclusion of the negotiation and a short post-negotiation analysis to see what happened and what can be improved for future negotiations with the vendor.

NEGOTIATION PHASE

- Opening
- Persuasion
- Agreement and review

Because you only get one chance to make a first impression, the first impression during the opening step is what will shape a vendor's expectations. So, try to take control of the negotiation in an assertive and subtle way during this period. This is the time to identify common ground with the vendor. This is also the perfect time to communicate expectations and obtain information from them. What is their range of negotiation? It is useful to assess how firm the vendor is in their arguments and any weaknesses you may find.

Once your position and the vendor's position have been identified and explained, it is time to move towards an agreement. By moving, we mean the give-and-take involved in negotiating and making concessions to the vendor to achieve an acceptable solution for both sides. Taking all this into account, you create a strategy that you will use during the negotiation.

Some methods of persuasion you can use during a negotiation are: emotion, by increasing the perceived value of the offer; logical arguments and evidence to demonstrate that the acceptable solution is the best one; and give-and-take which means the exchange of concessions on the table. We will always try not to expose our position and when we move, we will do it slowly and carefully.

Some influencing techniques I have previously used with vendors are: offering concessions that are not important for you, but very important for the vendor, such as shorter payment terms; informing the vendor that all other vendors have agreed to the proposal; and positively addressing the vendor's professional behaviour, performance or the relationship.

Breakthrough Approach

In some situations, we may find a vendor being negative or disruptive during a negotiation. Consider using William Ury's Breakthrough Approach:

If a vendor is being competitive, we should not react and we should distance ourselves mentally from their tactics.

If they are using negative emotions, we should disarm them by answering positively.

If the vendor is fixated in their argument, we should reframe the situation and offer them something they cannot resist.

If they think they can win without negotiating with us, we need to let them see that that is not the case and show them our other options, if necessary.

5.5.3. Post-negotiation Phase

It is the end of the negotiation and we have achieved an acceptable solution for both parties. Now, it is also important to discuss the next steps you are both going to take after the negotiation; specifically, what future business relationships will look like with the vendor. For example, if the vendor agrees to a lower rate in exchange for more work, you can set up a quick check-in for six months' time to make sure both parties are fulfilling the agreement.

This is an opportunity to gather additional information for future use and will help you create the review or post-mortem of the negotiation. This analysis can be used as a time to reflect, learn and measure the strength of the pre-negotiation phase and our performance during the negotiation. Focus on questions such as what went well, what could have been done better, any concession patterns visible on both sides and check if your assumptions became a reality.

Recording this information in the database can give the company an advantage next time there is a new negotiation with this vendor. As negotiation is also a part of the KPIs of the vendor management team, it is best practice to record the action in the team’s objectives to see how it might affect the company over time.

Chapter 6

Mastering the Pool: Management of Vendors

6.1. Management

The management of vendors is one of the main responsibilities of a vendor management team. This is an umbrella term that involves several tasks, so it takes most of the team's time on a regular basis. The management of vendors involves building and developing a relationship with them, establishing trust, so that the company can successfully complete all client requests. It also means the vendor management team is responsible for monitoring vendor performance, sometimes quality of work as well as communicating with them on a regular basis, and most importantly, overseeing conflict resolution.

When looking at the relationship, we would also consider whether a vendor is engaged by the company long-term, as an in-house or a retainer, for example a language lead or team lead of a group of translators for a certain language.

An in-house employee would be hired by the company while performing similar tasks to the vendors in the database. They would have the same rights and obligations as any other employee in the company.

A retainer position is offered to a freelancer when their services will be needed on a regular basis for a certain period of time. They will keep their freelance status, but will have a priority on your books when it comes to company projects. For example, two hours a day, Mondays to Wednesdays for a duration of 6 months.

These kinds of contracts are sought after because they provide the vendor's ensured availability for the company's projects. However, it is important to provide a regular stream of work, to avoid having the vendor on standby while waiting for the work to arrive. Not making the most of the time booked can lead to wasted company money and extra internal work from the team.

6.2. Vendor Performance and Quality of Service

General vendor performance should be monitored continuously to ensure the company is using the best vendors possible on each job. Collaborating regularly with a vendor that doesn't perform well continuously wastes time and money.

In general, the vendor management team takes care of monitoring a vendor's performance and sending performance feedback regularly. This can be good or bad feedback. Unfortunately, negative feedback is given much more often than positive, as it is thought to be more helpful than positive feedback.

This kind of feedback is usually related to their behaviour, meeting the company's expectations, and overall professionalism. Each company monitors performance differently. Therefore, the main areas that should be considered in a tracking system are communication, general availability, response time and personal traits that the company might consider crucial for the role of a vendor, such as welcoming feedback, politeness, flexibility, tech savviness, etc.

If the team doesn't have a tracking software for this data, I suggest using a field in the database profile. It is a comprehensive way to save the information, at the same time, it is available to anyone using the database at one glance. These notes should be dated and clearly written so employees can refer to them over time, even if they are not involved in the management of vendors.

In some companies, especially small ones, a vendor management team also takes care of monitoring the quality of vendors' deliveries.

This means tracking the amount and nature of the errors made on the jobs delivered to the client.

Quality of service is usually measured by a matrix and related to each task they complete, where the quality is scored with a number to make it easy to monitor. The task is sent for quality assurance, usually to another vendor to mark and amend any errors that might appear.

In my opinion, these matrices should also have a space for the assessor of the task to give positive feedback to the vendor being assessed as it usually only focuses on the errors. For example, for translation the team would follow LISA or TAUS quality standards to measure the quality of the vendor's service. Nowadays, there are new quality standards being created that match the needs of the current market, such as Multidimensional Quality Metrics.

Also, testing procedures, both entry tests and samples of work, are a way of measuring performance. The difference between a sample of work and an entry test is that the piece of work deliverable will be sent to revision before the entire project is completed. It is a useful way to send feedback to the vendor before delivering the final files. Samples of work can be done at any point of the collaboration as it depends on the quality process in place at the company.

6.3. Vendor Relationships

The relationship a company has with the vendor will affect levels of co-operation, meaning the amount of work the company sends to the vendor will impact the relationship and vice versa. Because each vendor is different, the vendor management team needs to understand the kind of business relationship the company holds with each vendor and how to develop it further.

It is important to note that the market is always changing with new additions and exits of vendors worldwide, and these changes are reflected in the database of a company. The vendor a company was outsourcing work to on a regular basis might retire, or a company's newly hired project manager may start to send regular work to a new vendor, because they are more like-minded. This is obviously not a recommended practice but, at the end of the day, we create human relationships while at work and it shows in different ways.

We need to examine the type of relationship the company holds with the vendor. This can be either a transactional relationship or a preferred vendor, maybe even a partnership in some cases. A transactional relationship is only based on the amount of work done by the vendor for the company. However, a preferred vendor, or a partner, are relationships where openness and trust is required by both parties long-term.

According to the European Language Industry Survey 2022, the vendors' satisfaction with their LSPs customers had an average score of 2.8 out of 4. Qualities most sought after by vendors when working with LSPs are reliability and professionalism, while partnership is last. However, these figures differ when it comes to vendors who work with direct clients. The survey shows that vendors value their role as a consultant and the importance of work quality as well as the flexibility and reliability offered.

These findings call our attention to an open secret in the industry: the gap between vendors and LSPs that has been expanding over decades. There is a big divide between vendor managers of LSPs who look to build a long-term collaboration and vendors wanting a transactional business relationship. This has been perpetuated after years of bad practice from LSPs towards vendors, where profit was prioritised over partnership.

I am glad to see the industry changing every day, setting higher standards and being more open about issues such as pricing and working conditions of members in the language services industry. Moreover, the introduction of a new wave of project and vendor managers valuing collaboration and professionalism over exploitation. I believe that even though we are building better relationships, there is still a long way to go until trust is restored between vendors and LSPs.

A few months ago, I tried to improve this situation by opening a thread on the Proz.com forum called *Anything and Everything About Vendor Management, Just Ask.* I thought it would be a great opportunity to talk honestly and openly about the interaction of vendor managers and vendors in the industry and for them to get to know our role a bit better. There were many comments asking for information, sharing frustrations and a bit of ranting. The questions span from what vendor management is to how translation-savvy should a vendor manager be and why vendor managers only contact vendors when they need to negotiate rates. Overall, I was quite pleased with the outcome.

6.4. Conflict Assessment

The Thomas-Kilmann Instrument is a tool used in conflict assessment. It states five possible approaches to negotiation, according to an individual's attempt to achieve their own objectives, here mentioned as assertiveness, versus satisfying the other party's objectives, here called co-operation.

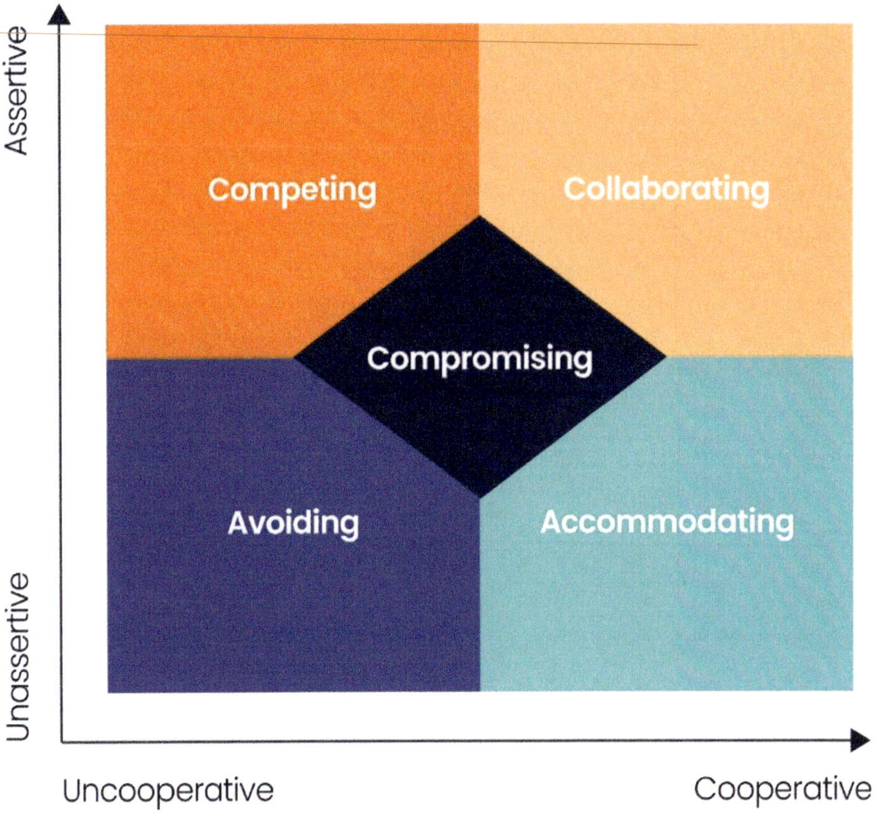

It suggests that if you are not ready to meet the company's objectives, nor those of the vendor, you should withdraw from the negotiation. For example, with a vendor that keeps getting in touch to establish a relationship every so often, but the company is not ready to take them on board, the suggested approach would be to avoid the request.

If, however, a company is very interested in working with a vendor, but the vendor is not very keen on working with the company, it suggests to accommodate the vendor's requests as much as possible to avoid losing the co-operation.

6.5. Vendor Engagement

According to the Oxford dictionary, engagement means to become involved, or have contact, with someone in an attempt to understand them. We refer to vendor engagement when we talk about the tasks that influence vendors to communicate and collaborate with the company proactively. This is a way to establish, develop and maintain the company's relationship with all their vendors. As we saw before, some vendors will take more time and effort from the vendor management team than others, so this is not a one-size-fits-all approach. For these techniques to be the most effective, they need to be tailored to the audience.

For example, it is not advisable to send an email mentioning the number of words the company has translated from English into Greek to those vendors that have been in the database for a while, but have never been used in a live project. However, it can be very beneficial to share those numbers with the vendors that were included in those projects to promote a sense of achievement and recognition for their work.

There are many ways to engage with vendors, but I will only share some of the ones I have encountered during my career. Vendor management teams all over the world are creating and implementing new ones every day.

The key is to think outside the box, be creative and ask vendors themselves how they would like to engage with the company. Recently, I learned about a colleague who once shared some details of her birthday presents during a Skype conversation with a vendor and since then, their relationship has evolved to the point where they exchange holiday pictures often and work together regularly.

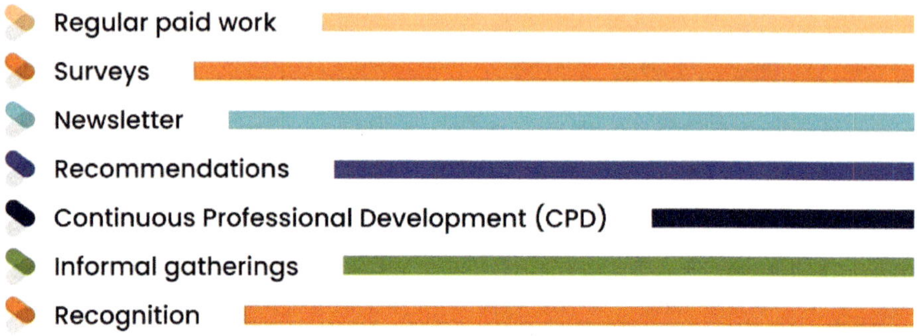

Regular Paid Work

This is probably the best way to engage vendors. Without regular paid work, it is very difficult to develop or maintain a relationship, as it is the basis of the collaboration between both parties.

Surveys

Apart from being a way to collect information, surveys are a great way to communicate with people in a creative way. It is better than emailing or calling because it allows you to gather information by only taking a few minutes from the vendors' time. To make it more enjoyable for vendors, use open questions, multiple choice, ratings, etc. Also, if you have a specific topic you would like to gather information about, you can create a question around it and add them in with more general questions. For example, if the company is looking to implement a new CAT tool across projects, you could create a question such as have you got any experience with the CAT tool memoQ? or how would you rate memoQ as a CAT tool?

- How many years have you been working with the company?
- How many projects have you completed during the last year?
- What do you enjoy most about working with the company?
- What do you least enjoy about working with the company?
- Would you recommend the company to other freelancers?
- Overall, how would you rate your collaboration with the company?
- What could our team do to improve our collaboration?

Newsletter

This is a timeless option, very much used by companies everywhere to engage with clients, vendors and followers. However, don't be fooled. It takes time and resources to write, format and distribute an interesting newsletter on a regular basis and one that won't be automatically moved to the junk folder.

Recommendations

I sent an email to some of our trusted vendors thanking them for their good work and asking if they wanted a recommendation from my company, either a letter of recommendation, a short review to publish on their website or a comment on LinkedIn. The initiative was very well received and 30% of the vendors replied. It only took me a couple of weeks to complete the task and many of them returned the gesture by rating the company on Proz.com, which was very appreciated and helped boost our rating and overall trustworthiness as a LSP in the market.

I know of some companies that don’t give referrals to their vendors. In my opinion, sharing vendors with another company is not a threat so long as the company can attract and engage the vendor in a way that encourages them to accept work from that company over work from others.

Continuous Professional Development (CPD)

Given the importance of CPD after the ISO 17:100 deployment, many vendors are keen on maintaining and developing their skills through courses, webinars, workshops, etc. Why not keep vendors engaged by offering interesting training? They will achieve their CPD objectives and the relationship will strengthen. These training sessions can be about anything and everything - from general software or industry practices to specific processes unique to your company. I personally love this idea, and I wish more companies would offer free training to their vendors on a regular basis. Continuous professional development is more important now than ever among vendors. Why not take advantage of it and organise some free training opportunities for suppliers and employees? In addition to learning something new, vendors will be able to interact with employees and other vendors. It can also improve the company's brand and consolidate the vendors' positive opinion of the company.

Informal Gatherings

Sometimes, emails can seem cold, and phone calls might be rushed to get the job done. Some years ago, Cecilia Iros talked at a GALA event about how they created a Facebook group for all their vendors where they can interact with the internal team to talk about anything but work. You might think Facebook groups are not what they once were nowadays so, what if we move the conversation to Zoom or Teams? Imagine a monthly networking session where vendors come into different breakout rooms and spend some time getting to know the team and talking about their pets, books or some other popular topic.

While working for Webcertain, I took the idea and created a Facebook profile through which vendors could interact with employees of the company. I posted industry news, company-related news and pictures of company events. It was quite entertaining and participants found it very interesting and fun. It helped them see past the corporate facade.

Now that people are starting to meet in person more often, what about a small informal event vendors can attend? I remember vendors coming to our head office to visit us some years ago, always a pleasant surprise. Creating an event for suppliers and employees is a great way for both parties to get to know each other better and interact in a different setting. Therefore, an opportunity for PMs and suppliers to mingle outside the office can be just what the company needs. It could even be done in the form of a quiz or themed party. Different groups can be strategically created to promote new translators and promising suppliers among the PM team.

Recognition

From a paper certificate to a box of chocolates or an Amazon voucher, recognition is a great way to promote engagement. Vendors love to know what clients think of their job. If you are unsure what categories to look at when ranking vendors, consider: who scored the best overall quality last month? Who accepted the most projects? Apart from making someone's day, it can also improve competition among suppliers.

6.5. Communication Skills

I don't want to delve deep into this topic here as the world is already full of resources where you can find out how to improve your communication skills. However, as mentioned previously, communication is key when it comes to vendor relationship and engagement, so let's look at the main things that should be taken into account for vendor management professionals.

Business communication should be warm and welcoming, but strong, meaning we need to be assertive and engaging, holding a polite, professional attitude with the vendor as well as being sound and secure in our message. Being perceived as disrespectful can affect our reputation as well as our company's, and it will damage our relationship with a vendor. Therefore, we will always try our best to value and respect vendors when communicating. At the end of the day, this business relationship is the result of interaction between human beings, so let's be kind to our fellow humans.

To develop and maintain a successful relationship with a vendor, we need soft skills, which focus on subjective, people-focused areas. I have divided them into two categories: interpersonal and intrapersonal skills. Interpersonal skills are used when interacting with other people, and intrapersonal focuses on our own thoughts and attitudes. Communication and negotiation are interpersonal skills, while self-awareness and management of emotions are intrapersonal skills. So, what should be taken into account when communicating?

Active listening: involves co-operating with a vendor to facilitate better understanding. For example, we will be alert and interested while encouraging them to speak openly, give feedback, and engage actively.

Questioning: we will use open and closed questions to apply pressure, give ultimatums, learn more, reflect back and even test the waters in some cases.

Cultural differences: it can be an issue when it comes to relationship approaches or negotiation styles. For example, some cultures use emotion when communicating to influence other people more than others and the use of formal and informal addressing is not always the same in different cultures.

Empathy: trying to understand other people's perspectives. Using vendors' names in email communication, or giving people your full attention during meetings are examples of empathic behaviour.

Assertiveness: stating one's views clearly and firmly without being aggressive. Using expressions such as "I understand you want me to take on this task, but I currently don't have the capacity for it."

Keep Swimming

One of the chapters of the first book I read about vendor management, Supplier Management by Jonathan O'Brien, started with this fun sentence, "To the supply base... and beyond!", a reference to the famous catch phrase from Buzz Lightyear in Toy Story.

I remember opening the book one evening after work, all my senses focused on those pages, ready to absorb all that I could from the words of a renowned procurement expert; then reading this title and bursting into laughter. Once I recovered and started reading again, a sense of purpose and fulfilment came over me and I think this feeling has been with me since. Why? Because it all starts with a database full of vendors and then it becomes so much more. It transforms into (business) relationships with different human beings, that opens our mind to different cultures and personalities, changing our perspective of the world.

Surely there are times where we want to give in to the vendors' demands and give up when our colleagues don't take our role seriously. It can be frustrating, and it is certainly not a job for the faint hearted. However, what keeps me going is knowing all the positive impact good vendor management has in every company. A good vendor management team can help the company run smoothly and more effectively by mitigating potential risks. They work together to ensure there are always enough vendors to cover the client's requests. They also help optimise vendors' performance, giving them feedback and keeping them engaged and interested in working with the company, creating long-lasting business relationships with vendors. Moreover, they monitor and reduce costs. Most importantly, the vendor management team protects and markets the company's brand to existing and potential vendors.

With the help of this book, you can implement all these benefits in your own company. A powerful leap forward in the way you do vendor management, more human and more driven. What is even better is that you can always come back to these pages for reference whenever you want. Refer back to the description of the role and its responsibilities, re-read the examples included and apply these procedures. Vendor management is a deep pool to dive into. Full of opportunities, rewards and unique challenges.

I hope this book becomes your essential industry guide and I can't wait to see how you take the tips and advice I have shared here to fuel your exciting future. Thank you for reading.

Were you inspired by some of these ideas and want to go a step further implementing your own version? Go ahead! Write to me at Carmen Cisneros on LinkedIn or carmen.cisnerosperez@outlook.com

About the Author

Carmen Cisneros started working in the translation industry in 2013 as a project coordinator. However, she soon realised vendor management was her passion. She has managed vendors in small, medium and large companies all over the world, building her expertise on how companies interact with their vendors and vice versa.

Nowadays, Carmen works as a vendor manager at Ultimate Languages in northern England. She also volunteers as the Education and Mentorship Manager for the Women in Localization UK chapter, as well as managing the Translation Vendor Management Group on LinkedIn, where vendor managers network and learn from one another. She has acted as moderator and public speaker for Women in Localization, Meet Central Europe and LSP Talk, among others.

Swimming Aids: Resources

LANGUAGE SERVICES INDUSTRY

Nimdzi Top 10 LSPs: https://www.nimdzi.com/nimdzi-100-top-lsp/

Slator Language industry Market Report:

https://slator.com/slator-2021-language-industry-market-report/

European Language Industry Survey (ELIS):

https://elis-survey.org/

NEGOTIATION

Power - Interest Grid:

https://www.projectmanagement.com/wikis/368897/stakeholder-analysis--using-the-power-interest-grid

William Ury' breakthrough:

https://www.williamury.com/the-five-steps-of-breakthrough-negotiation/

Negotiation in procurement:

https://www.cips.org/knowledge/procurement-topics-and-skills/strategy-policy/negotiation/

QUALITY

Translation quality evaluation from TAUS:

https://blog.taus.net/the-8-most-used-standards-and-metrics-for-translation-quality-evaluation

Testing:

https://www.linkedin.com/pulse/who-wants-test-forever-why-translation-tests-bed-roses-giada-gerotto/

https://blog.andovar.com/are-translation-tests-a-good-idea

Translation quality management and evaluation:

https://www.gala-global.org/events/events-calendar/translation-quality-management-and-evaluation-methodologies-lsps-and-buyers

VENDOR MANAGEMENT

Optimising vendor management:

https://www.slideshare.net/ceciliairos/optimizing-your-vendor-management

Successful translator recruitment:

https://www.atanet.org/resources/key-components-of-successful-translator-recruitment/#sthash.KkEityFl.TscVZcZ6.dpbs

Choosing a translator:

https://theatacompass.org/2016/01/05/how-to-choose-a-translation-vendor-9-tips-to-a-successful-experience/

Swim Practice Notes

Swim Practice Notes

Swim Practice Notes

Swim Practice Notes

Swim Practice Notes

Printed in Dunstable, United Kingdom

70549794R00067